I0711563

Nightly Letters
From me to me

Busola Shogbamimu

This journal belongs to:

Foreword

I am greatly humbled to write the foreword of this journal, and to present my bosom pal - Busola Shogbamimu,

Busola Shogbamimu is an ever grateful being who is always filled with smiles. This strong belief has driven her to write this journal and share with others. Her ardent attitude of appreciation has presented her with a life full of smiles.

She usually says "A grateful heart is a cheerful heart"

I have personally found that the reward to a life of gratitude is vast and knows no bounds. I believe that is the reason this journal is being presented to others to experience a life filled with smiles.

Olusola Okuwobi

Olusola Okuwobi is a Cyber Security Analyst who enjoys securing and guarding the information system from malicious attacks. She also works with children from diverse groups as an area representative of a Foreign Exchange Program.

A hearty cheer to you and a fulfilled LIFE

"Each new day is a brand new opportunity to improve yourself,
a gift to be appreciated, a choice to be a victor or a victim.
Wake up and decide."

-   **Busola Shogbamimu**

What is LIFE?

Legacy

Impact

Freedom

Empowerment

"Our greatest successes in life are often found in helping others succeed. Our most lasting and fulfilling achievements are often earned by helping others fulfill theirs."

I Am Me

In all the world,
There is no one else exactly like me.
Everything that comes out of me is authentically
mine,because I alone choose it.

I own everything about me – my body,
My feelings, my mouth, my voice, all my actions,
whether they be to others or to myself.

I own my fantasies, my dreams, my hopes, my fears.
I own all my triumphs and successes, all my failures
and mistakes.

Because I own all of me, I can become intimately
acquainted with me. By so doing I can love me and
be friendly with me in all my parts.
I know there are aspects about myself that puzzle me
and other aspects that I do not know; but as long as
I am friendly and loving to myself, I can
courageously and hopefully look for solutions to the
puzzles and for ways to find out more about me.

However I look and sound, whatever I say and do and whatever I think and feel at a given moment in time is authentically me.

If later some parts of how I looked, sounded, thought and felt turned out to be unfitting, I can discard that which I feel is unfitting, keep the rest, and invent something new for that which I discarded.

I can see, hear, feel, think, say, and do.
I have the tools to survive, to be close to others, to be productive and to make sense and order out of the world of people and things outside of me.

I own me, and therefore I can engineer me.
I am me

& I AM OKAY

By Virginia Satir

If you need more help in getting started on a life journey, send an email to Busola@rmlclubs.com today.

More books available on:
www.amazon.com/author/busolashogbamimu

Blog resources at:
www.busolashogbamimu.com

By Virginia Satir

If you need more help in getting started on a life journey, send an email to Busola@rmlclubs.com today.

More books available on:
www.amazon.com/author/busolashogbamimu

Blog resources at:
www.busolashogbamimu.com

"A life spent making mistakes is not only more honorable,
But, more useful than a life spent doing nothing."
George Bernard Shaw.

Dear God, Today I ...."

" Dear Me, Today I ...."

Dear God, Today I ...."

" Dear Me, Today I ...."

Don't worry and say, 'What will we eat?' or 'What will we drink?' or 'What will we wear?'

Dear God, Today I ...."

" Dear Me, Today I ...."

Dear God, Today I ...."

" Dear Me, Today I ...."

Each day

has

enough

trouble

of its

own.

Dear God, Today I ...."

" Dear Me, Today I ...."

Dear God, Today I ...."

" Dear Me, Today I ...."

Trust in the Lord
always and lean
not on your own
understanding

Dear God, Today I ...."

" Dear Me, Today I ...."

Dear God, Today I ...."

" Dear Me, Today I ...."

God's child solely
by; adoption.

#chosen

Dear God, Today I ...."

" Dear Me, Today I ...."

Dear God, Today I ...."

" Dear Me, Today I ...."

I stretch myself out. I sleep. Then I'm up again – rested, tall and steady.

Dear God, Today I ...."

" Dear Me, Today I ...."

Dear God, Today I ...."

" Dear Me, Today I ...."

You revive my drooping head; my cup brims with blessing.

" Dear Me, Today I ...."

Dear God, Today I ……….."

" Dear Me, Today I ...."

Dear God, Today I ...."

Real help comes
from God. Your
blessing clothes
your people!

Dear God, Today I ...."

" Dear Me, Today I ...."

Dear God, Today I ...."

" Dear Me, Today I ...."

Don't know how to
pray?
Just say it as it is.

Dear God, Today I ...."

" Dear Me, Today I ...."

Dear God, Today I ...."

" Dear Me, Today I ...."

*Unfailing love,
deeper than
oceans,
reaches to me.*

Dear God, Today I ...."

" Dear Me, Today I ...."

Dear God, Today I ...."

" Dear Me, Today I ...."

Everything I need, you supply.

Dear God, Today I ...."

" Dear Me, Today I ...."

Dear God, Today I ...."

" Dear Me, Today I ...."

Why are you worried about clothing? Have you considered the lilies

Mathew 6:28

Dear God, Today I ...."

" Dear Me, Today I ...."

Dear God, Today I ...."

" Dear Me, Today I ...."

saved only

by grace

Dear God, Today I ...."

" Dear Me, Today I ...."

Dear God, Today I ...."

" Dear Me, Today I ...."

Glow and flow!

No longer a slave
to fear

#washed by his blood

Dear God, Today I ...."

" Dear Me, Today I ...."

Dear God, Today I ...."

" Dear Me, Today I ...."

God said it.

I believe it.

That settles it!

Dear God, Today I ...."

" Dear Me, Today I ...."

Dear God, Today I ...."

" Dear Me, Today I ...."

Glow and flow!

No longer a slave
to fear

#washed by his blood

Dear God, Today I ...."

" Dear Me, Today I ...."

Dear God, Today I ...."

" Dear Me, Today I ...."

My father owns
the cattle on a
thousand hills.

#richkid

#kingdommatters

Dear God, Today I ...."

" Dear Me, Today I ...."

Dear God, Today I ...."

" Dear Me, Today I ...."

God's words does
not return to him
void, without
accomplishing the
purpose for which
it was sent.

Dear God, Today I ...."

" Dear Me, Today I ...."

Dear God, Today I ...."

" Dear Me, Today I ...."

A thousand years
is like one day.

#wait

Dear God, Today I ...."

" Dear Me, Today I ...."

Dear God, Today I ...."

" Dear Me, Today I ...."

God's love for me
has only one
description -

Reckless

#thoughundeserving

#beyondunderstanding

ILOVEIT

Dear God, Today I ...."

" Dear Me, Today I ...."

Dear God, Today I ...."

" Dear Me, Today I ...."

God is not a man
that he will lie.

Dear God, Today I ...."

" Dear Me, Today I ...."

Dear God, Today I ...."

" Dear Me, Today I ...."

When you go
through fire, you
will not be burned,
and the flames
will not harm you.

Dear God, Today I ...."

" Dear Me, Today I ...."

Dear God, Today I ...."

" Dear Me, Today I ...."

God's peace will stand guard over all your thoughts and feelings.

Dear God, Today I ...."

" Dear Me, Today I ...."

Dear God, Today I ...."

" Dear Me, Today I ...."

True to your word,
you let me catch
my breath and
send me in the
right direction.

Dear God, Today I ...."

" Dear Me, Today I ...."

Dear God, Today I ...."

" Dear Me, Today I ...."

You serve me a six-course dinner right in front of my enemies.

Dear God, Today I ...."

" Dear Me, Today I ...."

Dear God, Today I ...."

" Dear Me, Today I ...."

You hold my world
in your hands.

Dear God, Today I ...."

" Dear Me, Today I ...."

Dear God, Today I ...."

" Dear Me, Today I ...."

You have bedded me down in lush meadows; you find me quiet pools to drink from.

Dear God, Today I ...."

" Dear Me, Today I ...."

Dear God, Today I ...."

" Dear Me, Today I ...."

Your beauty and
love chase after me
every day of my
life.

Dear God, Today I ...."

" Dear Me, Today I ...."

Dear God, Today I ...."

" Dear Me, Today I ...."

At day's end I'm
ready for sound
sleep, For you,
God, have put my
life back together.

Dear God, Today I ...."

" Dear Me, Today I ...."

Dear God, Today I ...."

" Dear Me, Today I ...."

Everything I need, you supply.

Dear God, Today I ...."

" Dear Me, Today I ...."

Dear God, Today I ...."

" Dear Me, Today I ...."

Build up treasures in heaven.

Dear God, Today I ...."

" Dear Me, Today I ...."

Dear God, Today I ...."

" Dear Me, Today I ...."

2 meals = 40 days
strength.

#askElijah

1kings19

Dear God, Today I ...."

" Dear Me, Today I ...."

Dear God, Today I ...."

" Dear Me, Today I ...."

God's right hand
holds my right
hand

#donedeal

Dear God, Today I ...."

" Dear Me, Today I ...."

Dear God, Today I ...."

" Dear Me, Today I ...."

Nothing can
catch you by
surprise.

Dear God, Today I ....''

" Dear Me, Today I ...."

Dear God, Today I ...."

" Dear Me, Today I ...."

Great is your
faithfulness.

Dear God, Today I ...."

" Dear Me, Today I ...."

Dear God, Today I ...."

" Dear Me, Today I ...."

All must be well

Dear God, Today I ...."

" Dear Me, Today I ...."

Dear God, Today I ...."

" Dear Me, Today I ...."

I'm back home in
the house of God
for the rest of my
life.

Dear God, Today I ...."

" Dear Me, Today I ...."

Dear God, Today I ...."

" Dear Me, Today I ...."

You'll take afternoon naps without a worry, you'll enjoy a good night's sleep.

Dear God, Today I ...."

" Dear Me, Today I ...."

Dear God, Today I ...."

" Dear Me, Today I ...."

Shepherd of
my soul, I give
you full
control.

Daily Self- Declaration

I am _____________ *Your name*

I was born into a great family and I am pre-ordained by Almighty God himself to make a change in this life.

I am born for greatness and therefore I will fulfil my plan and purpose in this life

I am an achiever and a completer

I have gone through distractions and setback and I declare NO MORE

I am a strong man/woman with destinies to shape

I have been equipped with all that I need to make a difference

NOT A THING will hold me back

As I rise today, every step that I take drives me to my goal of divine and supernatural success

All that I lay my hands on today will prosper

I warmly receive fresh ideas and direction to achieve the task for today

Already lines are falling for me in pleasant places

Favour is lining the walls of every room I enter and so I will find favour before men and kings

I am abundance focused because I walk in prosperity and do not identify with lack

I am a quick thinker and an action taker an achiever and a completer.

Thank you, Father God for the gift of this new dayand the wisdom of heaven as

I ________Your name________________go out and WIN to the glory of your name.

(Copyright material)

Date ________________

Source of Anxiety ________________

Time ________________

Physical Sensations ________________

Place ________________

Negative Beliefs

About Yourself	About Situation

What facts do you know are true?

About Yourself	About Situation

Color where you feel
sensations of anxiety

Is there a more balanced way to think about this situation

What has helped before?

What is helping now?

Coping Mechanisms

Breathe
Remind yourself that anxiety is just a feeling
Describe your surroundings in detail
Go outdoors
Sip a warm or iced drink slowly
Ground yourself

Thank You For

Date

People To Pray For

Personal Challenges

Society And Government

Reflections

Playlist Title

Dedicated to ___________________________ Date _________

Song Name	Artist	Year	Notes

URL ____

Notes ____

Plant Name	**Date Planted**

Water Requirements 💧 💧💧 💧💧💧   Sunlight ☀ ◑ ●

☐ Seed   ☐ Transplant

Date	Event

Notes

Outcome

Uses

Purchased at: ________________________________   Price: ________________

Today's Goal ______________ Ⓜ Ⓣ Ⓦ Ⓣ Ⓕ ⬤S ⬤S

Muscle Group Focus ______________   Weight ________   Date/Time __________

Stretch ◯   Warm-Up ______________________________

Strength Training

Exercise		Set 1	Set 2	Set 3	Set 4	Set 5	Set 6
	Reps						
	Weight						
	Reps						
	Weight						
	Reps						
	Weight						
	Reps						
	Weight						
	Reps						
	Weight						
	Reps						
	Weight						
	Reps						
	Weight						
	Reps						
	Weight						
	Reps						
	Weight						
	Reps						
	Weight						

Cardio

Exercise	Calories	Distance	Time

Water Intake ______________

Cooldown ______________

Feeling ☆ ☆ ☆ ☆ ☆

Notes

	Mon	Tue	Wed	Thu	Fri	Sat	Sun
Bedtime							
Time Fell Asleep							
Daily Energy Level							
Last Thing Eaten							
Medication							
Last Activity							
Woke refreshed?							

Chart of Hours Slept

	Mon	Tue	Wed	Thu	Fri	Sat	Sun
7pm							
8pm							
9pm							
10pm							
11pm							
12pm							
1am							
2am							
3am							
4am							
5am							
6am							
7am							
8am							
9am							
10am							
11am							

Thank you for buying this journal and documenting your journal living lifestyle. Please share my amazon link with family and friends to access other books in my author's collection.

For feedback, you can drop me an email at busola@rmlclubs.com

My blog posts are live on:
www.busolashogbamimu.com

My books are available on:
www.amazon.com/author/busolashogbamimu

May we experience the sheer joy of fearless living, making trails and touching lives one day at a time.

xxxxxxxxxxxxxxxxxxxxxxxxxxxxxxxxxxxxxxxxxxxxxxxx